COMMUNITY
LIBRARY

Sunbury, Ohio

DONATED BY

SUNBURY–GALENA
ROTARY CLUB

DISCARDED

WEATHER

j369.43
Boy

BOY SCOUTS OF AMERICA
IRVING, TEXAS

109764

Requirements

1. Define meteorology. Explain how the weather affects farmers, sailors, aviators, and the outdoors construction industry. Tell why weather forecasts are important to each of these groups.

2. Name five dangerous weather-related conditions. Give the safety rules for each when outdoors and explain the difference between a severe weather watch and a warning. Discuss the safety rules with your family.

3. Draw cross sections of a cold front and a warm front showing the location and movements of the cold and warm air, the frontal slope, the location and types of clouds associated with the front, and the location of rain. Tell the differences between a cold front and a warm front.

4. Tell what causes wind, why it rains, and how lightning and hail are formed. Explain the difference between high- and low-pressure systems in the atmosphere and tell which is related to good and poor weather.

5. Identify and describe clouds in the low, middle, and upper levels of the atmosphere. Relate these to specific types of weather.

6. Draw a diagram of the water cycle and label its major processes. Explain the water cycle to your counselor.

7. Define acid rain. Identify which human activities pollute the atmosphere and the effects such pollution can have on people.

8. Do ONE of the following:

   a. Make one of the following instruments: wind vane, anemometer, rain gauge, hygrometer. Keep a daily weather log for one week using information from this instrument as well as from other sources such as local radio and television stations or

33274
ISBN 0-8395-3274-1
©1992 Boy Scouts of America
Revised 1996

10 9 8 7 6 5 4 3 2

NOAA Weather Radio. Record the following information at the same time every day: wind direction and speed, temperature, precipitation, and types of clouds. Be sure to make a note of any morning dew or frost. In the log, also list the weather forecasts from radio or television at the same time each day and show how the weather really turned out.

b. Visit a National Weather Service office or talk with a local radio or television weathercaster, private meteorologist, local agricultural extension service officer, or university meteorology instructor. Find out what type of weather is most dangerous or damaging to your community. Determine how severe weather and flood warnings reach the homes in your community.

9. Do ONE of the following:

a. Give a talk of more than five minutes to your unit explaining the camping safety rules in the event of lightning, flash floods, and tornadoes. Before your talk, show your outline to your counselor for approval.

b. Read several articles about acid rain and give a prepared talk of more than five minutes to your unit about the articles. Before your talk, show your outline to your counselor for approval.

Contents

Understanding the Atmosphere and Weather

Earth's atmosphere is a type of ocean. It's an ocean of air instead of water. Most human activities can be thought of as taking place at the bottom of the ocean of air in which we live.

The air is almost never at rest. Its restless movement is the source of everything people call the *weather.* The study of the atmosphere and its weather is the science of *meteorology.*

Many people think the word meteorology means the study of meteors. In a sense, it does. The word *meteor* comes from the Greek word for "thing in the sky." While most of us think of meteors as chunks of rock that fall from space, the word actually refers to anything that is a part of the atmosphere. Strictly speaking, clouds are meteors. So are raindrops, snowflakes, and hailstones. Even rainbows are meteors. And meteors are meteors, too. Meteorology involves the study of all things that relate to the weather.

Elements of the Atmosphere

The atmosphere is a mixture of *gases.* Six of the gases are present in amounts large enough to be important in the study of meteorology. Four of the six stay more or less in constant proportions, at least in the atmosphere's lowest 8 miles or so. The most abundant of these is *nitrogen,* making up about 78 percent. *Oxygen* is next, at about 21 percent, followed by *argon* at about 1 percent and *carbon dioxide* at about 0.03 percent. Three of these gases (nitrogen, oxygen, and carbon dioxide) are essential to life on Earth. If their proportions were to change significantly, all life would disappear.

The atmosphere contains two other important gases. Because their amounts change from time to time and place to place, they are called *variable gases.* One is *water vapor,* which can range from nearly zero to as high as about 4 percent of the total. Most of the water vapor is concentrated in the lowest mile of the atmosphere. When it condenses to form clouds, rain, and snow, it is the most important part of the weather.

The other variable gas is *ozone,* most of which is found above 6 miles. While ozone at sea level is harmful to humans and to plant life, its presence high in the atmosphere is important to our survival. Ozone in the upper part of the atmosphere shields us from the potentially harmful ultraviolet rays of the sun.

Atmospheric Layers

A cross section of the atmosphere shows that it consists of four main layers. There is no "top" to Earth's atmosphere. Instead, it gradually thins and merges with the very thin "atmosphere" of the sun.

The lowest layer of Earth's atmosphere is called the *troposphere.* This layer varies in depth from about 11 miles near the equator to only five or six miles over the north and south poles. The troposphere contains about 90 percent of the total mass of the atmosphere. It is within this layer that most of what we call "weather" occurs, and the mixture of gases described above stays nearly constant. Temperatures tend to decrease with height through the troposphere.

Above the troposphere is the *stratosphere.* This layer extends to a height of about 30 miles. In the stratosphere, the atmosphere is quite thin and the mixture of gases begins to change. Ozone is abundant in the lower part of the stratosphere.

The boundary between the troposphere and the stratosphere is called the *tropopause,* and is fairly well defined. At the tropopause, temperatures stop decreasing with height and begin to increase. This warming is due in part to the absorption of sunlight, which converts oxygen to ozone.

Above the stratosphere are two more layers called the *mesosphere* and the *thermosphere.* These layers are defined by how temperature varies with height, as shown in the diagram. They are not very important in most human activities.

However, another important "sphere" exists, called the *ionosphere.* It generally is found somewhere above the stratosphere. Because the air is so thin at this height, sunlight is much more intense than at the bottom of the earth's ocean of air. The strong

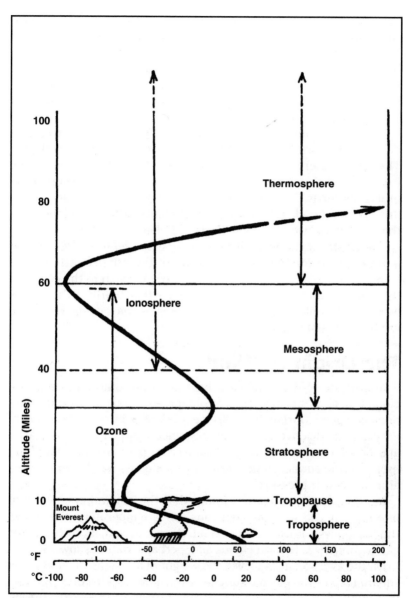

The basic atmospheric layers. Heavy solid line shows how temperature
changes with height.

sunlight strips *electrons* from gas atoms, creating *ionized* (electrically charged) particles. These charged particles are important because radio waves can "bounce off" the layers containing them. Normally there are several such layers, usually at heights of about 95 and 150 miles. These ionospheric layers move up and down during the daily cycle between day and night. Their height can affect long-distance radio communications.

The troposphere is constantly stirred by the motions that produce weather, which is why the mixture of gases is nearly constant. The stratosphere is not stirred as much. Since the drama of the weather is played out mostly in the troposphere, that is where meteorologists focus their attention. Here are spawned rain and snow, drought and flood, sandstorms and blizzards, wind and clouds—all the fair and foul weather that affects our plans and activities.

The depth of the troposphere, averaging about 8 miles, seems quite great to humans at the bottom of the atmospheric ocean. However, the distance from the surface of the earth to the center of the planet is about 4,000 miles. This means that nearly all the earth's weather takes place in a layer that is about as thick compared to the earth as is the skin of an apple.

The Origin of Wind

In prehistoric times, humans became aware that the weather—cloudy or clear skies, warm or cold air—depended on wind direction and speed. During the 1600s, people learned that air has weight. Researchers discovered that air becomes lighter when it is warm, and heavier when it is cold. Because the pressure that anything exerts on the surface of the earth depends on its weight, air temperature affects air pressure.

In addition, investigators found that the maximum amount of moisture air can hold also depends on its temperature: the cooler the air, the less moisture it can hold. If air is cooled, its stored water vapor condenses to form clouds and, perhaps, rain or snow.

On the average, at sea level, the weight of a column of air above a square inch of the earth's surface is 14.7 pounds. However, the fact that sunlight doesn't evenly heat the surface of the earth means that temperatures vary from place to place and time to time. Since warm air weighs less than cold air, warm regions tend to have lower pressures than cold places. This difference in pressure creates a force that makes the air move from high- to low-pressure regions, trying to equalize the pressure.

You are familiar with hot-air balloons. They rise when the air within them is heated. In the same way, if air in one place is heated in comparison to the air around it, that air tends to rise. As it does, air must flow in from around the heated region to replace the air that is rising.

If you live near a seacoast, you may see this process operate every day. During the day, the land heats more rapidly than the ocean. This heat warms the air over land and makes it rise. Cooler air from the sea flows in to replace it. In turn, the rising air over land flows out to sea at some level above the surface to replace the air flowing inland. This creates what is called a *sea breeze*.

At night, the opposite happens. The land cools more rapidly than the ocean. Air flows from land to sea at the surface, and the cycle is reversed. The circulation that results is called a *land breeze*.

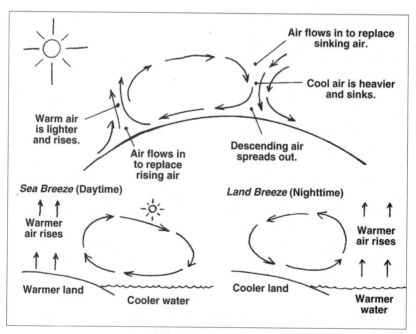

How winds are created

Similar circulations can develop around mountains, creating mountain and valley breezes. The winds that create the weather all arise in this way, as a result of unequal heating. However, it is not always this easy to understand why winds behave the way they do.

Global Wind and Pressure Systems

The global wind diagram on page 11 shows simplified wind patterns. The actual patterns of wind at any given moment are far more complicated than this, but the diagram shows the basic tendencies.

Warm air near the equator, in the *tropics,* tends to rise and flow toward the poles (poleward). Along the way, it cools and begins to sink. Because the equatorial regions are warm, they tend to form a belt of relatively low pressure. The regions of sinking air tend to be associated with relatively high pressure, in what are called the "horse latitudes" or *subtropics.*

(The reference to horses came about because sailing ships that entered this region of sinking air often met light winds and could be stranded for days. While the ships were stranded, the horses carried on board often died of dehydration. Dead animals were thrown overboard. If several ships were becalmed, the sea became littered with the bodies of horses; hence, the name.)

In a similar fashion, air over the poles tends to sink, being colder and heavier. This sends the air flowing into the *subpolar* regions, where it warms and rises, forming a belt with relatively low pressure at the surface.

The *middle latitudes,* where most of the United States is found, lie between the belt of subpolar lows and the subtropics. As shown in the diagram, air tends to flow poleward at the surface and toward the equator (equatorward) aloft, completing the transition between the polar and equatorial circulations.

Notice on the diagram how the surface winds blowing toward the equator in both hemispheres tend to come not directly equatorward, but shift to include a flow from east to west. Similarly, the surface winds blowing poleward tend to include a flow from west to east. Meteorologists refer to winds according to the direction from which they blow. Winds blowing from east to west are called *easterlies* and winds blowing from west to east are *westerlies.*

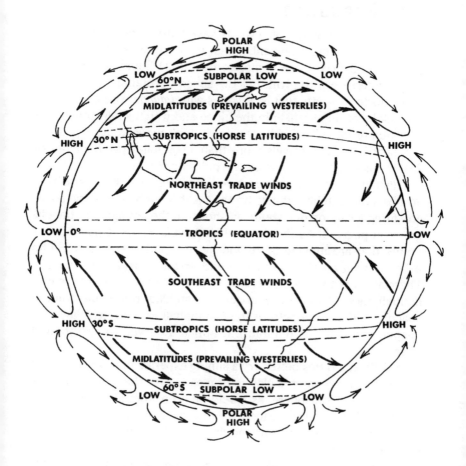

Global winds

If it weren't for the development of easterly and westerly winds, the tendencies for winds to blow straight from high- to low-pressure regions would be very similar to the local breezes described above. So what is the origin of the easterly and westerly winds in this global diagram?

The Relationship of Wind and Pressure

To understand why global winds have both easterly and westerly movement, you must remember that the earth is rotating about its polar axis. It makes one complete turn in 24 hours, which causes day to alternate with night. But the speed of rotation varies as you move north or south; that is, it varies with *latitude.* You can see this on a globe of the earth. Spin the globe and watch while points near the equator move fast while the poles don't move at all. A point on the earth's equator travels more than 1,000 miles per hour (about 25,000 miles in 24 hours), while the poles do not move.

This difference in speed produces an interesting effect as seen by an observer watching things on the earth's surface. Imagine someone firing a cannon due south, as shown in the left figure of the diagram on page 13. As the cannonball travels south, it passes over points that are moving more and more rapidly beneath it. So its path, *as seen on the earth* (the solid arrow), curves to the right. There appears to be a mysterious force making the path of the cannonball curve. Although an observer watching from some point in space would see the path of the cannonball as a straight line (the dashed arrow in the diagram), it appears curved to earthbound observers.

To understand this better, try a simple experiment. Turn a piece of paper steadily counterclockwise (the same way the earth rotates in the Northern Hemisphere, as would be seen from above the north pole). While turning the paper, try to draw a straight line on it. No matter which way you draw the line, it will end up curving to the right on the paper!

This apparent force, called the *Coriolis force* in honor of the scientist who discovered it, is very real to people living on the rotating earth. It must be accounted for when firing long-range artillery. It

Effect of Earth's rotation: the Coriolis force

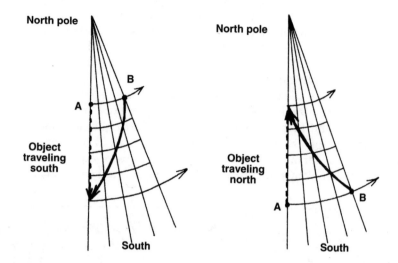

Origin (cannon) moves from A to B due to Earth's rotation. Object (cannonball) follows a curved path relative to the earth, with the path curving to the right (solid arrow). From space, an observer would see the object follow a straight line (dashed arrow).

affects rockets such as the space shuttle. Most importantly for the weather, it acts to make the moving air seem to curve to the right in the Northern Hemisphere and to the left in the Southern Hemisphere.

The Coriolis force varies with latitude just as the speed of rotation does. It is small near the equator and increases near the poles. This might seem strange, since the speed of the earth's rotation does exactly the opposite. The answer lies in the fact that the earth is a sphere, not a flat disk, and the rotation that counts is about the earth's axis, which passes through the poles. Most of what is described in this pamphlet about the effect of the Coriolis force applies best to areas poleward about 20 degrees north and south of the equator (that is, areas outside the tropics).

The strength of the Coriolis force on an object depends not only on latitude, but also on the speed of the moving object. As the speed of the object increases, so does the Coriolis force, so it makes sense that the effect would be more obvious the faster an object moves.

However, the amount of deflection also depends on the length of time over which the force acts. If the cannonball mentioned in the example above flies very fast and is in the air for only a short time, the effect will be small. For air, which moves at a fairly slow speed, the effect is quite small but the motion can continue for a long time. Therefore the Coriolis force can have a significant influence on air motion (winds).

As you have seen, unequal heating can create regions of relatively high and relatively low pressure. Low-pressure regions (called *cyclones*) and high-pressure regions (*anticyclones*) are shown on weather maps using contours. Most Scouts should be familiar with the idea of terrain contours, which are lines of equal elevation. When you look at a map with terrain contours, you can visualize the

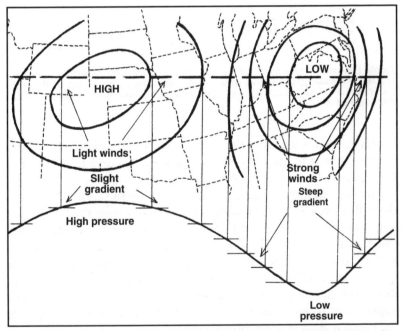

Isobars (lines of equal pressure) around high- and low-pressure areas are farther apart in areas of lighter winds and closer together in areas of stronger winds. Distribution of pressure along the dashed line is shown on the bottom graph, revealing the steeper "slope" of the pressure gradient on either side of the low-pressure center.

variations in elevation. You can see the variations in pressure on a weather map in the same way. The pressure contours (called *isobars*) are lines of equal atmospheric pressure.

Now, recall that where terrain contours are close together, the land slopes more steeply. In the same way, you can see that in a region where the isobars are closer together, the pressure difference (or *pressure gradient*) is greater over that region. And just like terrain, where things tend to move downhill, air tends to flow "downhill" from high to low pressure. Air moves faster where there is a greater pressure gradient, just as a ball rolls faster down a steep slope than on a nearly level surface.

Consider what happens to the air within a cyclone. Air tends to move toward the low-pressure region of the cyclone. But as it does, it is deflected to the right (in the Northern Hemisphere) by the Coriolis force. The air speeds up, but the increase in speed results in an increase in the Coriolis effect. This means that the amount of deflection also is increasing, so the air follows a path that turns more and more to the right of its original direction. Eventually, it can reach a state of balance where the effect of the pressure difference is exactly balanced by the deflection arising from the Coriolis effect. This state of balance is called *geostrophic* balance, from the Greek meaning "earth turning."

This rather idealized picture of the wind means that winds blow parallel to the isobars, with a speed determined by the isobar spacing. The closer together the isobars, the faster the winds. The air tends to rush into low-pressure regions and fill them, but the Coriolis force deflects the air. Air then circulates around the lows (cyclones) and highs (anticyclones) instead of deflating the highs and filling the lows.

The actual wind flow is altered constantly by factors like unequal heating, so real winds in the atmosphere are only approximately in geostrophic balance. But you can see that if the wind were exactly in geostrophic balance, the flow would be counterclockwise around a low and clockwise around a high in the Northern Hemisphere, as shown in the diagram. In the Southern Hemisphere the direction is reversed—clockwise around lows and counterclockwise around highs. Real winds do indeed tend to do this, especially higher in the air above the disturbing influence of the earth's surface.

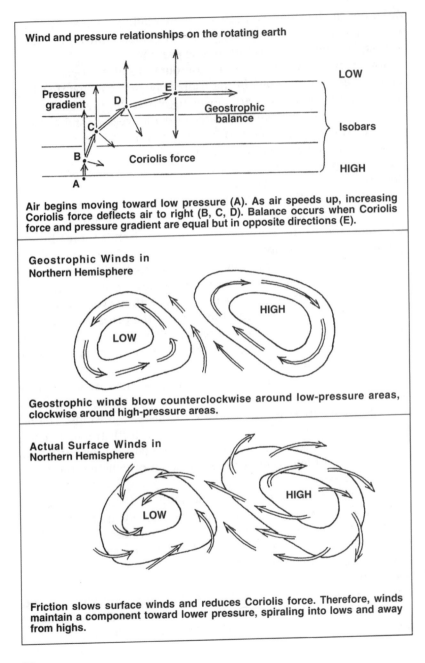

Wind and pressure relationships on the rotating earth

LOW

Pressure gradient

Geostrophic balance

Isobars

Coriolis force

HIGH

Air begins moving toward low pressure (A). As air speeds up, increasing Coriolis force deflects air to right (B, C, D). Balance occurs when Coriolis force and pressure gradient are equal but in opposite directions (E).

Geostrophic Winds in Northern Hemisphere

HIGH

LOW

Geostrophic winds blow counterclockwise around low-pressure areas, clockwise around high-pressure areas.

Actual Surface Winds in Northern Hemisphere

HIGH

LOW

Friction slows surface winds and reduces Coriolis force. Therefore, winds maintain a component toward lower pressure, spiraling into lows and away from highs.

At and near the surface, another factor comes into play. Within the lowest 3,000 feet of the atmosphere (about one kilometer), the friction caused by the earth's surface slows the speed of the wind. It can't go quite fast enough to balance the force caused by pressure differences. Therefore, winds near the surface usually maintain some of their motion toward lower pressure. This results in winds that spiral into a cyclone and out of an anticyclone (see the diagram).

Now do you better understand the global wind picture near the surface shown earlier? Air moving out of the subtropical high-pressure belts (around 30 degrees latitude) spirals anticyclonically (clockwise, in the Northern Hemisphere), while air moving into subpolar low-pressure regions (near 60 degrees latitude) spirals cyclonically (counterclockwise).

Moisture—The Hydrologic Cycle

The most important thing about the weather is the moisture it brings. The wind could blow night and day and the temperature could rise and fall, but if no rain fell, Earth would be in real trouble. Mars is a planet like that.

Fortunately, in addition to a wonderful air-circulating system, the earth has a wonderful water-circulating system. The water vapor that forms clouds and precipitation comes mostly from *evaporation* from the earth's oceans. A small part comes from lakes, streams, and *transpiration* of green plants.

Most of the rain that falls over land evaporates and is *transported* as water vapor by the winds, often many thousands of miles from its source. Water vapor *condenses* into clouds and falls back to the earth as *precipitation* (rain, snow, etc.). Some precipitation joins the *runoff,* which is water that flows in rivulets and streams to the rivers. Part of the precipitation *percolates* into the ground to replenish the *groundwater* supply, which also feeds the rivers. Some groundwater is taken up by plants and animals, which breathe it back into the atmosphere through the process known as transpiration.

Some precipitation falls as snow. Of this, most eventually melts and joins the runoff or percolates into the groundwater. However, part of the snowfall remains frozen, locked into slow-moving rivers of ice called *glaciers.* A considerable amount of the earth's water supply is tied up in the form of ice over the polar regions of the globe, especially Antarctica. The ice gradually moves in glaciers toward the ocean, but it may take hundreds or thousands of years for water that falls as snow over glaciers to reach the ocean.

A small amount of the groundwater becomes trapped in the earth, forming underground reservoirs called *aquifers.* In many parts of the world, including the United States, the water in aquifers is tapped for human use, especially for irrigation. Once the aquifers are drained, it may be many thousands of years before they fill again.

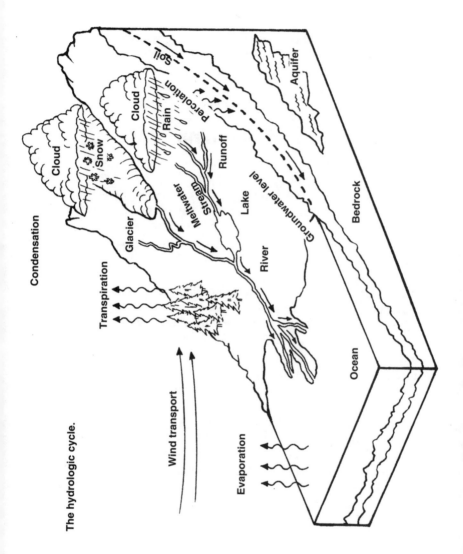

The hydrologic cycle.

Condensation

Transpiration

Wind transport

Evaporation

Cloud

Snow

Cloud

Rain

Glacier

Meltwater

Stream

Soil

Percolation

Runoff

Lake

River

Groundwater level

Aquifer

Bedrock

Ocean

19

Polar ice packs, glaciers, and underground aquifers tie up some of the earth's water supply, but overall, water that evaporates from the oceans eventually finds its way back to the oceans. All of the events described above—evaporation, transpiration, water vapor transport, condensation, precipitation, runoff, percolation, and streamflow—are part of a cycle of events known as the *hydrologic cycle*. On the whole, the cycle is in balance. That is, the total amount of water on the planet remains constant.

Humidity and Dewpoint

The water vapor content of the air is called *atmospheric humidity*. Air that contains the maximum amount of water vapor possible is said to be *saturated*. That maximum amount is not constant. It varies with the temperature of the air. Warmer air can hold more water than cool air. This means that air can reach saturation either by the addition of water vapor (through evaporation or transpiration) or by cooling.

On a clear night, the temperature of the air near the ground may fall until saturation is reached. The air continues to cool, to the point that it can no longer hold all the water vapor. Some of the water is forced to condense onto objects on the ground, forming *dew*. Under the right conditions, *ground fog* can form. Condensation in the atmosphere usually is caused by this process—cooling the air to saturation. Only rarely is condensation in the atmosphere caused by adding water to the air through evaporation at the same temperature.

The air temperature at which saturation takes place when the air pressure stays constant is called the *dewpoint temperature* (or just *dewpoint*). If the air already is saturated, the air temperature and the dewpoint are the same. The dewpoint shows directly how much moisture is in the air—the more moisture, the higher the dewpoint.

While the dewpoint often remains more or less constant during the day, that is not so for another, more common measure of atmospheric moisture: *relative humidity*. Relative humidity is the ratio of the actual amount of water vapor in the air divided by the maximum amount it can hold at that temperature. It usually is expressed as a percentage.

You probably have heard radio and television announcers give the relative humidity as a part of the weather report. If the relative humidity is 50 percent, it means that the air contains one-half of the total amount of water vapor needed to saturate it. But remember that when the air temperature rises, so does the total amount of water vapor it can hold. Therefore, if the actual amount of water vapor stays the same, the relative humidity decreases when the temperature rises, and increases when the temperature falls.

In hot weather, humans sweat to stay cool. The evaporation of water absorbs heat from the body. If the air is near saturation, sweating is not very effective at cooling us, so we feel uncomfortable.

Relative humidity reports can be deceiving about comfort. On a summer evening when the temperature goes down, we feel more comfortable than during the heat of the day, even though the relative humidity actually increases as the temperature falls. Human comfort depends more on the dewpoint than on the relative humidity. Summer days can be uncomfortable when the dewpoint rises above 60°F even though the relative humidity at the time of the maximum daytime temperature can be low.

At a temperature of 95°F and a dewpoint of 65° the relative humidity is only about 35 percent, but it will feel hot and muggy. If the dewpoint remains the same and the temperature drops to 70° after dark, the relative humidity will rise to almost 85 percent but it will feel more comfortable than it was during the day.

Forms of Precipitation

Precipitation generally falls from clouds, but not always. *Fog* is merely a cloud forming at the earth's surface. It occurs most frequently at night along streams and swamps where the cooling of slow-moving air combined with the source of moisture pushes the air to saturation. In the winter or spring, warm moist air flowing in over cold land areas may be cooled to its dewpoint temperature, resulting in a widespread area of fog. Also, when cold air moves over warm water, the water evaporating into the cold air can increase the dewpoint temperature of the air to saturation, resulting in widespread fog.

When fog is blown by the wind against objects with surface temperatures below freezing, a type of ice deposit called *rime* is formed. The fog particles, which can remain liquid down to temperatures of about -40°F, freeze upon contact with the object and build up a white deposit. (A similar deposit may build up in some refrigerator freezers.) The white or milky appearance of rime ice is due to small regions of air that are trapped between the fog particles before they freeze.

Frost occurs when air's dewpoint is below freezing. The condensing water vapor is deposited in feathery patterns of ice crystals instead of tiny droplets. The object it forms upon must also be below freezing, but the air from which it condenses may be several degrees above freezing. It is not uncommon for solid objects to cool below freezing in low-lying areas on nights when the temperature is close to but slightly above freezing.

Precipitation from Clouds

Fog, rime, and frost aside, most forms of precipitation are associated with clouds. Clouds form when water vapor condenses to form ice crystals or water droplets in the air. Cloud formation generally is associated with rising air. Rising air cools as it ascends because pressure decreases with height. The drop in pressure causes the rising air to expand and the expansion results in cooling the air. Eventually, the ascending air is cooled to its dewpoint and condensation begins.

The condensed particles, either ice or water, are so tiny that turbulent air motion holds them aloft. As more and more water vapor condenses, some of the particles collide with each other and merge to form droplets large enough to begin to fall. As they fall, they continue to grow by sweeping up smaller droplets along the way—a process called *coalescence*. When droplets become just large enough to fall to the surface, they are called *drizzle*. It may take a thousand or more cloud droplets to form a single drop of drizzle. As the droplets continue to grow, they reach a size large enough to be called *rain*. Rain is the simplest and most common form of precipitation in middle latitudes.

Snow is not frozen rain. It is made up of ice crystals condensing directly from water vapor without any liquid stage. Snow forms when cloud temperatures are well below freezing. It can form and fall even when temperatures at the surface of the earth are above freezing. If surface temperatures are warm enough, however, the falling snow will melt and fall as drizzle or rain. Melting snowflakes usually are small enough to become drizzle, but sometimes snowflakes clump together and form small white pellets called *graupel* (pronounce the "au" like "aw" in "crawl").

Sometimes a layer of warm air lies above cold air near the ground. Rain falling from the warm air into the cold surface air can cool to a temperature below freezing but remain liquid. Raindrops in this state are *supercooled*. When this supercooled rain or drizzle falls on a cold object at the surface, it freezes instantly, resulting in *freezing rain* or *freezing drizzle*. Sometimes the raindrops freeze before reaching the ground, creating ice pellets or *sleet*. Sleet and freezing rain can fall at the same time as some raindrops freeze while others remain supercooled.

One of the most spectacular forms of precipitation is *hail*. Hail is the result of ice forming in the rising currents of air, or *updrafts*, of thunderstorms. When an updraft is strong enough, it holds the ice aloft. Many layers of supercooled water freeze to the ice, adding to its size. These layers can be seen in the cross section shown in the photograph. They give the hailstone a structure like an onion.

Cross section through a hailstone, showing layers of ice.

The hailstone grows until the updraft can no longer hold it aloft, or until its motion within the storm carries it out of the updraft. Then it falls to the earth, perhaps melting somewhat as it nears the warm air near the surface. Hailstones can range from the size of small peas to as large as grapefruits. Large hailstones often are not simple spheres, but take on irregular shapes as a result of being tossed and turned within the turbulent air of the thunderstorm.

Visibility

Visibility indicates the transparency of air. Air contains particles that reflect and scatter light, so that objects at a distance can't be seen. Smoke from fires, dust picked up over land, and salt particles from evaporated ocean spray can be carried great distances by wind and can collect in still areas. Water droplets in the form of clouds or fog also can reduce visibility. So can raindrops and snowflakes if there are enough of them.

To determine visibility for meteorological reasons, an observer looks for several objects whose distances from the observing point are known. By noting the distance of the farthest object that can be seen, visibility can be estimated. Visibility is normally reported in miles or a fraction of a mile.

Visibility is essential in aircraft operation and in navigating almost any kind of transportation vehicle (cars, trucks, and especially planes and boats). Observations of visibility are routinely reported all over the world.

Fronts

In radio and television weather reports, you often hear about *fronts*. An announcer might say something like "A warm front is coming up the coast" or "A strong cold front is moving down from Canada." These reports sound as though an invasion were on the way. In a sense, that's right. The reports are describing the invasion of *air masses.*

Air masses form when air remains in place over a particular region for several days. The air gradually takes on the characteristics of the surface beneath it. For example, air over tropical oceans becomes warm and moist, while air over snow-covered polar regions becomes dry and cold. When the air moves away from the place where it formed, known as its *source region,* it replaces air of a different type. The boundaries between air masses of different types are what meteorologists call fronts. Fronts are regions of transition, and often are where important weather events take place.

Air masses usually are associated with high-pressure regions (anticyclones) at the surface. Low-pressure regions (cyclones) dominate on the boundaries of air masses. By increasing the winds and pushing the air away from its source, the development of cyclones causes air masses to move away from their source regions.

When cold air replaces warmer air, the front is called a *cold front.* In the United States, cold air usually comes from the north or northwest from Canada and the polar regions. Because cold air is more dense than warm air, it tends to stay nearer the surface and wedges beneath the warm air. This tends to make the warm air rise, as seen in the diagram. The rising air cools by expansion, forming clouds and perhaps precipitation.

Because the advancing cold air remains near the surface where friction is a factor, the movement of the cold air is slowed somewhat by the friction near the ground. This creates a steep slope along the leading edge of the front. The slope can mean that most of the rising motion along the front is confined to a narrow zone near the front.

When warm air replaces cold air, the front is called a *warm front.* Warm air masses form over the warm tropical oceans south and southeast of the United States and over land areas to the southwest. Those forming over oceans are moist. Those forming over land are dry. When warm air approaches a cold air mass, it tends

109764

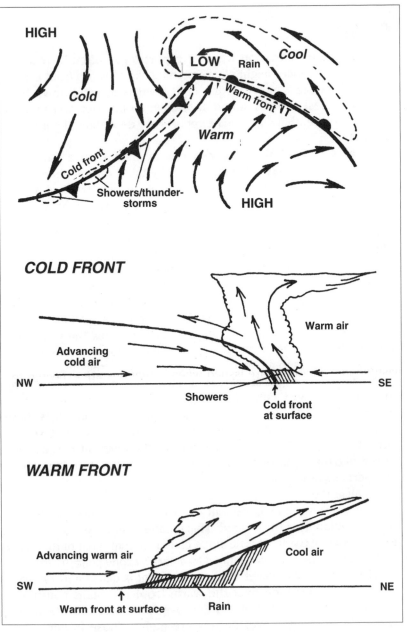

Warm and cold fronts

to ride up over it rather than wedging beneath it. Unlike cold fronts, therefore, warm fronts tend to have gentle slopes. As the warm air rises and cools, clouds and precipitation may form. The shallow slope means that rain and clouds can precede the passage of a warm front by a day or more.

Severe Weather

People readily adapt to routine weather changes that occur with the passage of air masses. Sometimes, however, the weather can become so violent that unusual precautions are needed. The sections below describe some weather events that require special precautions and offer safety tips.

Forecasters with the National Weather Service issue watches, warnings, and advisories to alert the public to potentially violent or hazardous weather. There is an important difference between a watch and a warning. A *watch* means that hazardous weather is possible, or that conditions are favorable for it to develop. A *warning* is a more urgent notice that hazardous conditions already exist or are heading your way. Watches and warnings are issued for events such as winter storms, tornadoes, severe thunderstorms, high winds, and flash floods. *Advisories* are issued when conditions are expected to cause serious inconveniences. A common type of advisory alerts motorists to hazards such as slippery roads caused by wintry weather.

Winter Storms

During the winter, some cyclones (low-pressure areas) develop into unusually intense storms that bring heavy snow, strong winds, and cold temperatures. When the wind is strong enough (above 35 miles per hour) and visibility is reduced to less than a quarter mile by snow or blowing snow, the event is termed a *blizzard.* Even if a storm doesn't quite qualify as a blizzard, a combination of snow, wind, and cold can be deadly for people caught unprepared.

Another winter event that can be quite severe is freezing rain (or drizzle), or an *ice storm.* If ice builds up thickly enough, tree branches begin to break, often crashing into power and telephone lines already burdened with ice. Roads become ice-covered and dangerous.

WIND CHILL TABLE
Equivalent temperature in cooling power on exposed flesh

Wind Speed MPH	Air temperature (degrees Fahrenheit)													
	35	30	25	20	15	10	5	0	-5	-10	-15	-20	-25	-30
0-4	35	30	25	20	15	10	5	0	-5	-10	-15	-20	-25	-30
5	32	27	22	16	11	6	0	-5	-10	-15	-21	-26	-31	-36
10	22	16	10	3	-3	-9	-15	-22	-27	-34	-40	-46	-52	-58
15	16	9	2	-5	-11	-18	-25	-31	-38	-45	-51	-58	-65	-72
20	12	4	-3	-10	-17	-24	-31	-39	-46	-53	-60	-67	-74	-81
25	8	1	-7	-15	-22	-29	-36	-44	-51	-59	-66	-74	-81	-88
30	6	-2	-10	-18	-25	-33	-41	-49	-56	-64	-71	-79	-86	-93
35	4	-4	-12	-20	-27	-35	-43	-52	-58	-67	-74	-82	-89	-97
40	3	-5	-13	-21	-29	-37	-45	-53	-60	-69	-76	-84	-92	-100
45	2	-6	-14	-22	-30	-38	-46	-54	-62	-70	-78	-85	-83	-102

Wind speeds greater than 40 mph have little additional chilling effect

Even without snow or ice, extreme cold can be dangerous. Bitter cold can be even more hazardous when accompanied by high wind because the two increase the rate of heat loss from exposed skin. The results can be *frostbite,* which is damage to skin from freezing, and *hypothermia,* a lowering of body temperature.

Meteorologists use *wind chill* to describe the combined effect of cold and wind. Wind chill temperatures always are the same as or lower than the actual temperature, and decrease with higher winds. For example, with a temperature of 30°F, the wind chill also is 30° if winds are nearly calm, but drops to 4° if winds are blowing at 20 mph.

If you are caught outdoors in a winter storm or in extreme cold, it is important to stay dry, cover all exposed parts of your body (several layers of clothing provide more protection than a single heavy coat), and avoid overexertion. These precautions will help to prevent frostbite and hypothermia. If there is no shelter available, prepare a lean-to, windbreak, or snow cave for protection from the wind. Build a fire if possible. A fire will provide heat and might help to attract the attention of rescuers. Rocks placed around the fire will help to absorb and reflect heat. One other tip: Always melt snow for drinking, rather than eating it to quench thirst. Using your own body heat to melt snow will lower your body temperature.

Thunderstorms

Thunderstorms are most common in the tropics and subtropics and during the warm season in middle latitudes, but they can occur in winter and at polar latitudes. They form when warm, moist air creates updrafts that, in turn, form large precipitation drops in clouds. As this precipitation develops, *positive* and *negative* electrical charges are separated and build up in different parts of the clouds. Similar areas of charge develop on the ground beneath the clouds. When charges have built up enough, they can "jump the gap" between regions of opposite charge, discharging the areas.

This discharge is what we see as *lightning.* Some lightning flashes strike the earth but most are from one part of a cloud to another. Lightning ground strikes are fairly common events in most parts of the United States. They can be killers for those who are unprotected.

Most lightning flashes are from one part of a cloud to another.

Thunder is caused by the great heat generated during the brief time (less than a second) that a lightning discharge occurs. The heat causes the air to expand rapidly, as in an explosion.

Sound travels at a speed of 1,100 feet per second, but light travels at a speed of about 186,000 *miles* per second. Therefore, you will see a lightning flash almost instantly, but the sound of thunder will take longer to reach you. You can use this difference to estimate the distance to the flash. Count the seconds it takes for the sound of the thunder to reach you after you see a lightning flash. Since a mile is 5,280 feet, it takes thunder about 5 seconds to travel 1 mile.

Although the location where lightning will strike is not predictable, some places are much more likely to be struck than others. Because lightning follows the path of least resistance, objects closer to the cloud are more likely to be struck. Trees in an otherwise open space often are targets for lightning, so trees are not a good place to take shelter in a thunderstorm.

If you are caught outdoors in a thunderstorm, do not stand in open areas or near lightning targets like trees, power poles, or wire fences. When hiking near mountaintops, which can be struck by lightning nearly every day during summer, get downhill before the lightning begins, if possible. If you're caught by a storm, take shelter in a cave or a low spot among the rocks. Remove any metallic frame packs and do not stay near them.

A steel-framed building or motor vehicle often is a safe place because the charge stays within the frame, which conducts it safely to ground without danger to the occupants. Do not use the telephone or hold objects connected to electrical power (like hair dryers) during a thunderstorm. Staying near stoves, fireplaces, and plumbing also is dangerous.

Though lightning can be hazardous, it is not all bad. It changes the air's nitrogen into a form that can be taken up by plants. Thus a thunderstorm can be a natural plant fertilizer as well as a waterer.

Thunderstorms can become quite violent, producing large hail, flooding rains, strong winds, and tornadoes. These severe thunderstorms tend to occur with strong cyclones. During the winter, a single cyclone can produce blizzards, ice storms, and severe thunderstorms with tornadoes in different locations all at the same time.

Floods

Floods are an unavoidable part of life along rivers. The torrential rains of thunderstorms or tropical cyclones can cause flooding. Some floods occur when winter or spring rains combine with melting snows to fill river basins with too much water too quickly. Such events usually take several days to develop. Other floods arise suddenly as the result of heavy localized rainfall. These *flash floods* can become raging torrents very fast, perhaps in less than an hour, and can sweep away everything in their path.

Areas of rugged terrain are particularly vulnerable to flash floods. Picturesque river valleys in the mountains can be swept without warning by floods from rains falling some distance away. When camping, stay clear of natural streambeds during the time of year when rainstorms are common. If you camp on low ground you might be caught unawares, especially when asleep at night. In case of a flood in rugged terrain, climb to high ground immediately, even if it means abandoning your gear. Do not get into motor vehicles and attempt to drive away from the flood danger. Never enter a flooded low spot on the road or trail if you do not know how deep the water is, especially if the water is rising.

Keep alert to signs of wet weather—not just in your location, but also in nearby areas. Listen for distant thunder and watch for lightning flashes. Faster flowing streams or rising water levels can signal rainfall upstream. In seasons when heavy rains are possible, at least one person in your group should carry a portable radio and stay informed about weather conditions when in range of a radio station. When out of radio range, be keenly observant and alert to the weather.

Tornadoes

On rare occasions, rapidly rotating columns of air form within a thunderstorm. When these rotating columns reach the earth's surface, they become *tornadoes*.

Tornadoes can produce the strongest winds on earth, occasionally reaching 300 miles per hour or more. The tornado is an extreme form of cyclone, with very low pressure at its core. (The core pres-

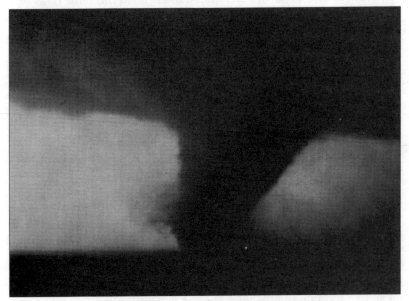

Tornado near Seymour, Texas, on April 10, 1979

sures in tornadoes have never been measured accurately—measuring devices do not survive such events easily.) Most tornadoes produce paths of damage that are only a few hundred yards wide or less. Because tornadoes usually last only a few minutes, path lengths typically are a mile or less. A few tornadoes, however, can be more than a mile wide and can last for an hour or more, producing damage paths more than 100 miles long.

Most tornado casualties are caused by flying debris, so the best thing to do if a tornado threatens is to get to a place that provides as much protection from flying debris as possible. Avoid trees; they become a source of debris in tornadoes. (You already know that taking shelter from thunderstorms near a tree is not a good idea, because of the lightning danger.) If you are caught in the open when a tornado approaches, get to a low spot, lie face down, and cover your head. As with floods, never attempt to drive away from a tornado. You are likely to be trapped in your vehicle, which is an extremely dangerous situation.

Tornadoes can occur while you're in school or at home. Be aware of any plans for tornado safety in your school. You and your family should develop a safety plan at home. If your home has a tornado shelter, use it. If your home has a basement, it can be a good shelter if part of it is protected from falling debris, such as under a stairway or a heavy workbench.

If you can't get to a tornado shelter or basement, put as many solid walls between you and the outside as possible. Closets in interior hallways are good shelters. Bathrooms often have stronger walls than the rest of the house because the plumbing makes a kind of reinforcement. Stay away from windows—flying glass is extremely hazardous. Abandon mobile homes and seek nearby shelter. Take along a radio and some source of fresh water. If your home is hit, be alert to leaking gas from broken pipes.

Hurricanes

Among the most dangerous storms that affect the United States are *hurricanes*. They originate in the southern part of the north Atlantic Ocean, the Caribbean Sea, the Gulf of Mexico, and in the southeastern Pacific Ocean off the west coast of Mexico. Similar storms occur elsewhere in the world, notably in the oceans near

Satellite photograph of Hurricane Norman in the eastern Pacific Ocean near the Baja Peninsula in early September 1978

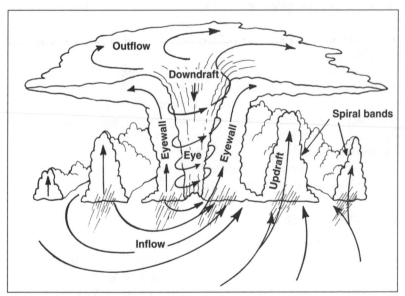

Cross section showing the structure of a typical mature tropical cyclone

India and Australia, where they are called *cyclones,* and in the western Pacific Ocean, where they are called *typhoons.* A general name for all such storms is *tropical cyclone.*

Unlike the low-pressure systems of middle latitudes, tropical cyclones contain no fronts because they form in a single, tropical air mass. When well developed, they are nearly circular in shape and vary in diameter from 100 to around 1,000 miles. In rare instances their winds can exceed 200 miles per hour, spiraling inward to the low-pressure center. The combined effects of the winds and the low pressure act to pile up ocean water in the center of the storm, producing what is called the *storm surge.* As the storm approaches land, the storm surge can combine with normal tides to produce extensive flooding. It is the storm surge, not the wind, that causes the most damage and the most casualties from hurricanes. Most hurricane deaths are by drowning.

At the center is the *eye* of the storm, which can range from about 5 to more than 20 miles in diameter. Within the eye, winds are light and only low clouds might be present. Skies actually might be clear within the eye. Surrounding the eye is a ring of deep clouds called the *eyewall.* The strongest winds in the storm usually are found within the eyewall next to the relatively calm eye. Several cloud bands made up of lines of thunderstorms, called *spiral bands,* usually are present in a tropical cyclone. They spiral into and join the eyewall from the outer parts of the storm. Torrential rains often accompany the eyewall and the spiral bands. Most hurricanes also produce occasional tornadoes from the thunderstorms in the spiral bands.

Tropical cyclones "feed" on warm tropical ocean waters. This is how they obtain their strength over the open waters of the tropics, and why they normally weaken rapidly and soon dissipate after they meet land. But even a dissipated hurricane can produce extremely heavy rainfall, sometimes well inland from the point where it made landfall.

In nearly all cases, hurricane watches and warnings will precede any landfalling hurricane. If you are camping along or near a seashore when hurricane watches are issued, strike camp and leave the area immediately. Encountering a hurricane at sea also is extremely dangerous and should be avoided at all times.

Cloud Formation

Clouds are classified according to their heights and forms. The highest clouds, generally above 20,000 feet, are called *cirrus* clouds, meaning hairlike or curly. Cirrus clouds are composed entirely of ice crystals because of the low temperatures at the heights where they form. Cirrus clouds that form in lumpy clumps are called *cirrocumulus* (*cumulus* means a heap or pile). Cirrocumulus clouds can be arranged in patches or aligned in rows. Cirrus clouds forming in extensive flat layers are known as *cirrostratus* (*stratus* means a layer). Cirrostratus clouds can cover the whole sky or only part of it, and can be quite thin and nearly transparent, or thick and opaque.

The middle group of clouds, with heights roughly between 10,000 and 20,000 feet, has the prefix *alto-*, meaning high, before each cloud name. This group includes *altocumulus,* which is the middle-cloud equivalent of cirrocumulus. Altocumulus clouds also can appear in patches or in rows. There are *altostratus* clouds, which appear flat and layered in large patches. Altostratus clouds occasionally can cover nearly the whole sky, but can be thin enough to let the sun show through dimly. Sometimes the sun can be seen through altocumulus clouds as if through a piece of frosted glass.

Low clouds appear from near the earth's surface up to about 10,000 feet. *Stratus* clouds appear as a uniform cloud layer, with little or no texture. (Fog can be thought of as a stratus cloud at the surface.) Low-level *cumulus* clouds, generally with flat bases and rounded tops, are indicators of fair weather. However, sometimes cumulus clouds develop upward into deep, towering thunderheads known as *cumulonimbus* clouds. Cumulonimbus clouds can be more than 50,000 feet tall and almost always flatten out near the tropopause. *Stratocumulus* clouds combine the features of stratus (flat) and cumulus (heaped) clouds. They typically are flat and nearly uniform at their bases but puffy and clumped on top.

Fair Weather Cumulus Clouds
When these fluffy "cloud ships" are floating in an azure sky, they are called fair-weather cumulus, and they usually mean good weather is ahead.

Cirrus Clouds
Very high, wispy clouds, composed of ice crystals are called cirrus, meaning hairlike or curly.

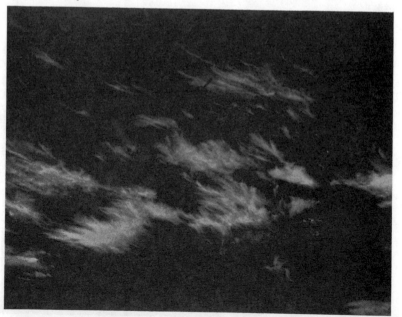

Cirrostratus Clouds
These hazy, thin clouds are like a cloud-veil over the sky, high up. They are fairly transparent, showing any sunlight or moonlight above.

Altocumulus Clouds
Like flocks of sheep, some white and some gray, the altocumulus clouds cover the sky with a fluffy blanket. They can be distinguished by the rounded contours of the clouds with small openings showing blue sky above and by their height.

Altostratus Clouds
These high, dense clouds usually bring steady rainfall, although the rain is often lighter than the heavy clouds seem to indicate.

Stratus Clouds
A sign of bad weather are the low-lying stratus clouds that seem to hang above the ground like a dense curtain of fog.

Cumulonimbus Clouds (forming)
If you see cumulus clouds piling up to windward like the ones in this picture, you will know that they are likely to change into cumulonimbus storm clouds.

Cumulonimbus Storm Clouds
This is a full-fledged cumulonimbus cloud that is a typical thunderstorm in the making. It will likely bring lightning, heavy rain, and possibly hail if it is to windward. The anvil top is a good identification mark of this type of cloud.

Stratocumulus Clouds
Somewhat like to altocumulus but lower, darker, and thicker are the stratocumulus. They are likely to be in long, heavy ridges like corrugated roofing.

Measuring and Recording the Weather

Accurate information about the various factors that together define the weather is necessary in making reliable forecasts. For each of these factors, there is an instrument that measures intensity, velocity, or degree.

Air Pressure

Air pressure is measured using a *barometer.* You can make a simple mercury barometer from a glass tube about a half inch in diameter and a yard long. Seal one end of the tube and fill it with mercury. Then cover the open end with your finger and invert the tube in a cup or dish of mercury. Be careful not to let any air into the tube. When you remove your finger, the mercury column will fall to a level that measures the atmospheric pressure. Air pressure acts on the surface of the mercury in the cup or dish, forcing the mercury up into the tube. The higher the air pressure, the higher the level of mercury in the tube. Be very careful when handling mercury. It is a deadly poison if swallowed, even in small amounts.

Another kind of barometer, the *aneroid* barometer, is the type you are most likely to have at home or see in stores. Instead of a mercury tube, it uses a small thin-metal "box" sealed with average air pressure inside. The box contracts under high pressure and expands when the outside air pressure drops. An indicator needle is attached to the side of the box by levers and records the pressure on a dial.

Barometers, either aneroid or mercury, are read in terms of the height in inches of a column of mercury. Average air pressure at sea level corresponds to a column of mercury about 30 inches tall. This is where the barometer reading comes from on weather reports—a pressure of 30.25 inches, for example. Air pressure at sea level

Downward air pressure on mercury in bowl forces mercury up into tube. The higher the air pressure, the higher the mercury column.

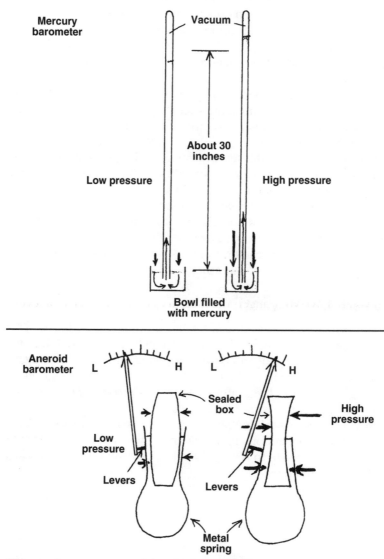

Changes in pressure result in changes in width of sealed box. Levers and springs convert these changes into pressure readings.

varies by only a small amount. A reading of, say, 31 inches is unusually high, while a reading below 29 inches occurs only in the strongest cyclones, such as hurricanes.

The exact height of the mercury column depends not only on air pressure, but also on the altitude where the reading is taken. To adjust for differences in elevation, it is common to correct the readings for altitude so that the measurements are comparable to those taken at sea level.

On actual weather maps, pressures are converted to *millibars,* the scientific unit in which pressure is measured. The numbers on the isobars on a weather map correspond to pressure adjusted to sea level, in millibars.

The rate at which the air pressure is changing often is more important than the pressure reading itself. Air pressure rises typically with the approach of high pressure and its attendant fair weather. So if you hear the weather announcer say, "The barometric pressure is 29.65 inches and rising," you can be pretty sure that good weather is on the way. Likewise, the approach of a low-pressure area causes the reading to fall. When sailors say "the glass is falling," they look for poor weather.

Wind Direction

You probably have seen *wind vanes* on houses and barns. They are all pretty much alike, although they can be decorated differently. Most are in the form of an arrow that pivots on special bearings so that it can turn freely in the wind. It is accurately balanced on the bearing. The size of the feather part of the arrow is larger so that wind vanes always swing into the wind and point in the direction from which the wind is coming. A professional wind vane usually has electrical connections to a scale in the weather office so that no one has to go outside to read it. Weather reporters do know enough to stay out of the rain!

A simple wind vane

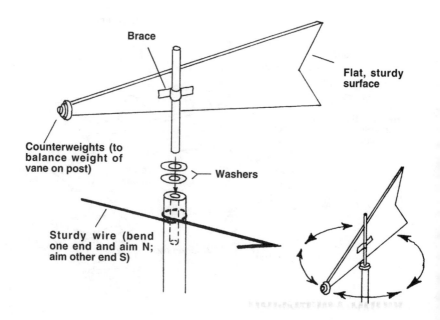

Brace

Flat, sturdy surface

Counterweights (to balance weight of vane on post)

Washers

Sturdy wire (bend one end and aim N; aim other end S)

Wind Speed

Wind speed is measured by an instrument called an *anemometer.* Here are two designs for making your own. The first works much like official instruments. Once you build this kind of anemometer, you can listen to your local radio or television station to convert your readings into measurements. Wind speeds can be measured in miles per hour, in *knots,* or in meters per second. A knot is one *nautical mile* per hour, which is slightly faster than an ordinary mile per hour because a nautical mile is about 6,080 feet, roughly 15 percent longer than an ordinary mile of 5,280 feet. Miles per hour normally are used in the weather reports you hear on radio and television, while knots are used mostly in marine and aviation weather reports. Most scientific measurements are in meters per second.

The other type of anemometer is a simple plate type. It is acceptable for the merit badge requirements.

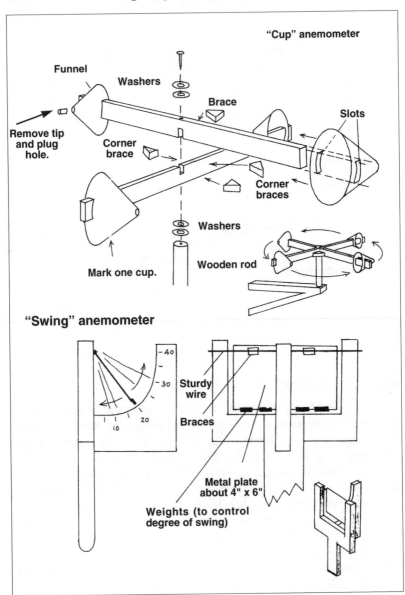

"Cup" anemometer

Funnel

Washers

Brace

Slots

Remove tip and plug hole.

Corner brace

Corner braces

Washers

Mark one cup.

Wooden rod

"Swing" anemometer

40

30

20

10

Sturdy wire

Braces

Metal plate about 4" x 6"

Weights (to control degree of swing)

BEAUFORT WIND SCALE

Beaufort Number	Description	Wind speed (MPH)	Observations (Visible effects on land)
0	Calm	less than 1	Smoke rises vertically
1	Light air	1–3	Direction of wind shown by smoke drift, but not by wind vanes
2	Light breeze	4–7	Wind felt on face; leaves rustle; ordinary vanes moved by wind
3	Gentle breeze	8–12	Leaves and small twigs in constant motion; wind extends light flag
4	Moderate breeze	13–18	Raises dust and loose paper; small branches are moved
5	Fresh breeze	19–24	Small trees in leaf begin to sway; crested wavelets form on inland water
6	Strong breeze	25–31	Large branches in motion; whistling heard in telegraph wires; umbrella difficult to use
7	Moderate gale	32–38	Whole trees in motion; inconvenience felt in walking against wind
8	Fresh gale	39–46	Twigs break off trees; progress generally impeded
9	Strong gale	47–54	Slight structural damage; branches break
10	Whole gale	55–63	Considerable structural damage; trees uprooted; seldom experienced inland
11	Storm	64–72	Widespread damage; very rarely experienced
12	Hurricane	above 72	Extreme damage

This scale was devised by Sir Francis Beaufort in 1805. Although used mainly to estimate winds at sea, the visible effects described here relate to land-based observations.

Air Temperature

Air temperature is an important factor in weather, especially when associated with other factors such as humidity and pressure. It is measured with a *thermometer*. In most of the world, temperatures are measured in degrees Celsius, but in the United States surface air temperatures are measured and reported in degrees Fahrenheit. Water freezes at 32° Fahrenheit (F) but at 0° Celsius (C). Water boils at 212°F but at 100°C.

For most of the United States, 40° below zero (which reads the same on both the Celsius and the Fahrenheit scales) to 110°F (about 43°C) is a range of temperatures wide enough to cover most temperature observations. In Death Valley, California, however, the temperature once soared to 134°F, while in Yellowstone National Park the temperature has been known to sink to 66°F below zero. In such places, you need a special thermometer.

The most accurate thermometers are the liquid-in-glass-tube type, containing either mercury or alcohol. The alcohol type is most appropriate for very cold places because alcohol freezes at a lower temperature than mercury.

A thermometer should be kept in the shade and away from wind and rain. The weather professional's thermometer is housed in a ventilated box raised above the ground and protected from the weather.

Water Vapor

A common instrument for finding out the amount of water vapor in the air is the *wet-bulb hygrometer*. It is relatively easy to make. Begin by purchasing two identical liquid-in-glass thermometers. These can be bought in hardware stores for a reasonable price. Mount both thermometers on a milk carton, as shown, exactly the same distance from the bottom. Cut off about 6 inches of a new white shoelace, trimming off the tip. Slip the shoelace over the bulb portion of one of the two thermometers. Cut a slot in the milk carton so that you can slip the bottom part of the lace into the carton. Fill the carton with water up to the slot. If possible, use distilled or filtered water because impurities in the water will cause inaccurate readings.

Wet-bulb hygrometer

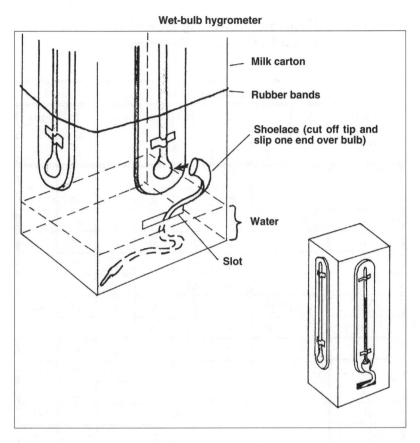

Milk carton

Rubber bands

Shoelace (cut off tip and slip one end over bulb)

Water

Slot

Place the carton in the breeze of an electric fan or in a breezy open window. Make sure the shoelace is wet up to the thermometer bulb. Evaporation of water from the lace will cause the temperature measured by the wet-bulb thermometer to decrease, while the other thermometer should remain at the actual air temperature.

Using the following chart, you can figure out the relative humidity by the temperature difference between the two thermometers. When they both read the same, or nearly so, expect wet weather because that means high (nearly 100 percent) relative humidity. Generally, the wet-bulb temperature is somewhere between the actual air temperature and the dewpoint temperature discussed earlier.

Table of Relative Humidity Based on dry-Bulb (Air) and Wet-bulb Temperatures

Difference (Dry-bulb minus wet bulb)	Dry-bulb (air) temperature, Fahrenheit							
	30	40	50	60	70	80	90	100
1	88	92	93	94	95	96	96	-
2	77	84	87	89	90	92	92	-
3	67	76	80	84	86	87	89	-
4	57	68	74	78	81	83	85	-
6	37	53	62	68	72	76	78	80
8	17	38	50	58	64	68	71	74
10		23	39	49	56	61	65	68
12		9	28	40	48	54	59	62
14			17	31	41	48	53	57
16			7	23	34	41	47	52
18				14	27	35	42	47
20				7	20	30	37	42
22					14	24	32	38
24					7	19	27	33
26					1	14	22	29
28						9	18	25
30						4	14	21

Table of relative humidity based on dry-bulb (air) and wet-bulb temperatures. Using this table, compare readings on a wet-bulb thermometer with those on a dry-bulb thermometer to determine relative humidity. Check the degree difference shown on your two thermometers. Find this number in the left column of the table and read across to the column under the air (dry-bulb) temperature. The value shown is the relative humidity. Example: If the difference between dry- and wet-bulb temperatures is 6 degrees and the air temperature is 70 degrees, the relative humidity is 72 percent.

Rainfall

Rain is measured with a *rain gauge.* We measure rain in terms of the depth of the layer it would make if none drained off or was otherwise lost. In the United States, rainfall is measured in inches to the nearest hundredth. An amount too small to measure is called a *trace.*

Rainfall can be measured in many ways, but usually a large funnel and narrow receptacle are used. The figure shows a simple tin-can type of rain gauge that you can make and use.

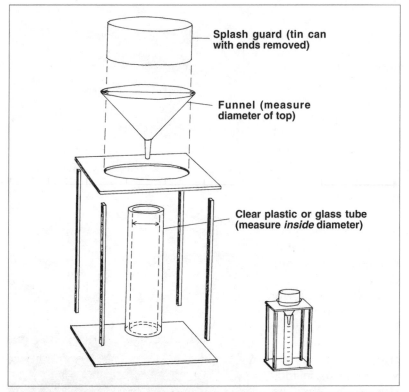

Rain gauge. Rainwater funnels into a narrow tube so that amounts can be read more accurately. Measure the diameters of the opening and the tube and calculate their ratio. Mark off the tube using the square of that ratio. For example, if the opening is twice as wide as the tube, then 4 inches (2 times 2) in the tube will mean 1 inch of rainfall. If the ratio is 3 to 1, then 9 inches (3 times 3) will equal 1 inch of rain, and so forth.

Weather Maps

The various elements described above including temperature, pressure, wind, and precipitation are measured at weather stations all over the world at specified times each day. Observations usually are made every 6 hours at all land stations and aboard ships at sea.

Weather observations are prepared using a short code of numbers and are transmitted electronically to major weather centers. The contents of these reports are plotted on surface weather maps, mostly by computers. In addition to the surface reports, information is gathered around the world on weather elements aloft by balloon-borne instruments called *radiosondes,* usually every 12 hours. The radiosonde reports (or data) also are plotted on weather maps for various levels in the atmosphere. All this information is exchanged with similar reports from other countries and used in preparing weather charts for forecasting.

Every day in the United States, the National Weather Service prepares and transmits many weather maps. In addition to showing the data, the maps have many lines drawn on them. Similar to terrain contours, these

A radiosonde instrument package attached to a balloon is about to be released by a National Weather Service meteorologist to sample the temperature, humidity, pressure, and winds aloft.

lines connect points of equal values of weather elements. Isobars, discussed earlier, are lines of equal pressure. Lines of equal temperature are called *isotherms*. Other features may be included on weather maps such as fronts, precipitation, visibility, and cloud types. These elements normally are indicated by special symbols.

The information transmitted to the major weather centers also is entered into computers and used to generate computer "models" of the atmosphere. These models are different from physical replicas such as model cars. Atmospheric models exist only as a bunch of numbers in a computer. Weather observations are entered into the computer and processed through mathematical formulas to make what are called *Numerical Weather Prediction* (or NWP) forecasts. NWP forecast information is sent back to the weather offices to be used by weather forecasters.

By using current weather information at the surface and aloft, combined with satellite images of clouds, data from weather radars, and NWP forecasts, meteorologists can make fairly accurate predictions about the weather systems affecting their areas of forecast responsibility. It has been shown that even if meteorologists had perfect models of the atmosphere, there are practical limitations on how well they could forecast the weather. This is because it's not possible to take perfect measurements at every point within the entire atmosphere. Obviously, weather models are not perfect. As everyone knows, forecasts sometimes are wrong. However, progress has been made. Today's forecasts for *three* days in advance are about as accurate as those made twenty-five years ago for *one* day in advance.

Study One Week's Weather

The best way to learn about weather maps is to look at a few. Following are examples of daily weather maps issued by the National Weather Service at the same time each day for one week. Study them carefully. They tell much about one week's weather. On them, isobars are marked in millibars. Where the lines are far apart, winds tend to be weak. Where they are close together, winds generally are strong.

Note the symbols for the winds at each station. The wind barbs show the direction from which the wind is blowing. The flags and lines show the speeds. A half line is 5 knots, a full line is 10 knots, and a flag is 50 knots. As you can see, the winds around lows tend to spiral counterclockwise, while those around highs go clockwise.

Temperatures are shown in degrees Fahrenheit. Below the temperatures are dewpoint temperatures, also in degrees Fahrenheit.

How to Read a Weather Map

The surface weather maps on the following pages show plotted station observations and analyses of pressure, temperature, and front locations at 7 a.m. eastern standard time. The station reports shown are only a fraction of those on which the analyses are based. Other reports are not plotted here because of lack of space. An example of a plotted station is shown on page 55. Study this example and compare it with the actual reports on the maps to find station temperatures, winds, pressure, 6-hour rainfall, etc.

Cold fronts are shown as heavy solid lines with triangles pointing in the direction in which the cold air is advancing. *Warm fronts* are shown as lines with solid semicircles pointing in the direction toward which the warm air is moving. Fronts with alternating triangles and semicircles pointing in opposite directions are *stationary fronts*. Neither the warm air nor the cold is moving very much, so these fronts are hardly moving at all. Sometimes a cold front will overtake a warm front, creating an *occluded front*. Occluded fronts usually extend from strong, well-developed cyclones. They are shown with alternating triangles and semicircles pointing in the same direction.

Contours of equal pressure, or *isobars,* are shown as solid lines and are labeled in millibars. Centers of high pressure (anticyclones) and low pressure (cyclones) are indicated by high and low, respectively. Note on the maps how surface winds generally spiral counterclockwise into cyclones and clockwise away from anticyclones. The tracks of well-defined cyclones are shown by a chain of arrows, with previous cyclone center locations shown by small black squares with white crosses. Thick dashed lines show elongated areas of low pressure, or low-pressure *troughs*.

Areas of precipitation are indicated by shading. Lines of equal temperature *(isotherms)* are shown for 32°F (thin dashed line) and 0°F (dash-dot line).

Actual weather maps vary in detail from the maps shown. Simpler versions usually appear in newspaper and television weather reports, while maps analyzed by weather forecasters often are much more detailed. But general features (such as fronts) are shown similarly on most maps using standard symbols much like those seen here.

Surface maps and the station model below were provided by the National Oceanic and Atmospheric Administration (NOAA), National Weather Service, Climate Analysis Center.

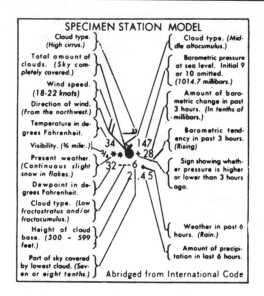

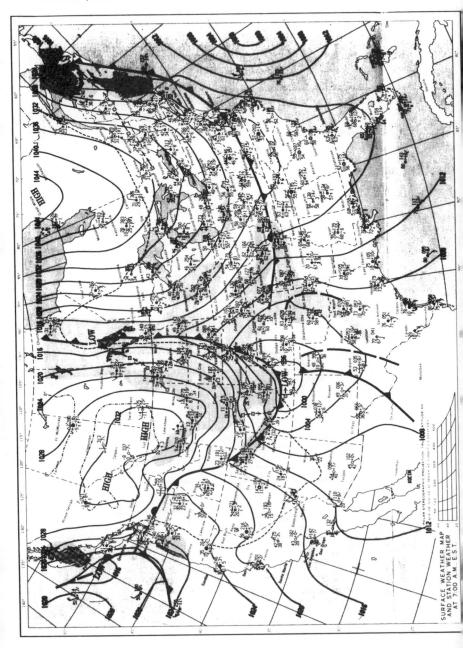

SURFACE WEATHER MAP
AND STATION WEATHER
AT 7:00 A.M. E.S.T.

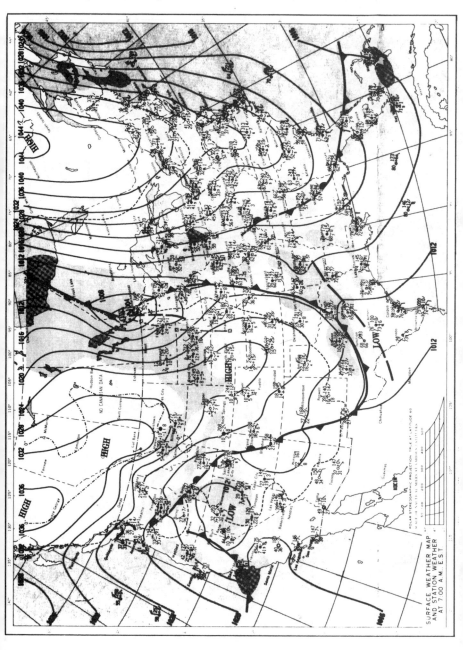

SURFACE WEATHER MAP
AND STATION WEATHER
AT 7:00 A.M. EST

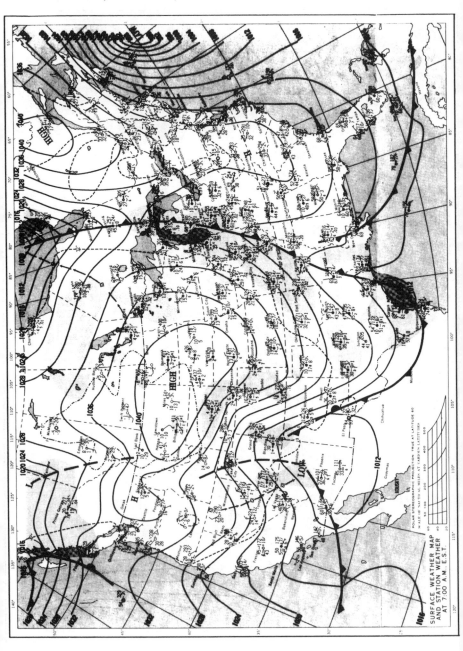

SURFACE WEATHER MAP
AND STATION WEATHER
AT 7:00 A.M. E.S.T.

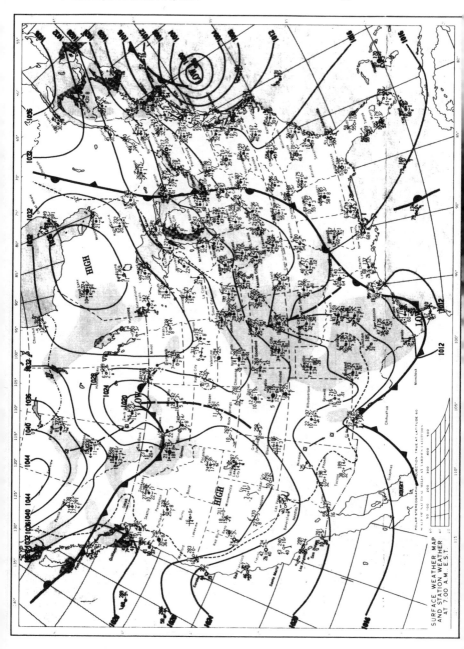

SURFACE WEATHER MAP
AND STATION WEATHER
AT 7:00 A.M. E.S.T.

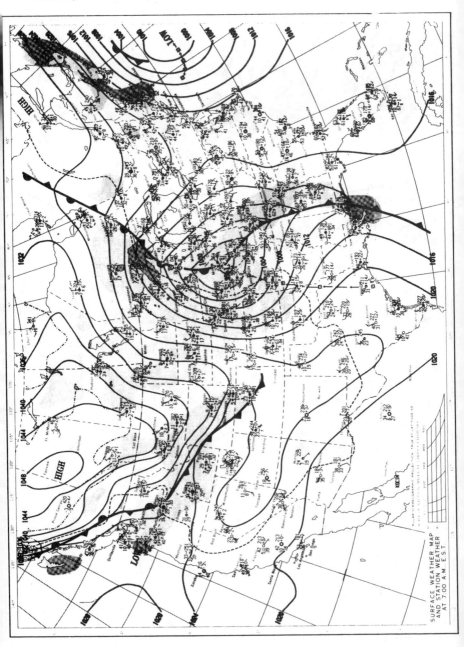

SURFACE WEATHER MAP
AND STATION WEATHER
AT 7:00 A.M. E.S.T.

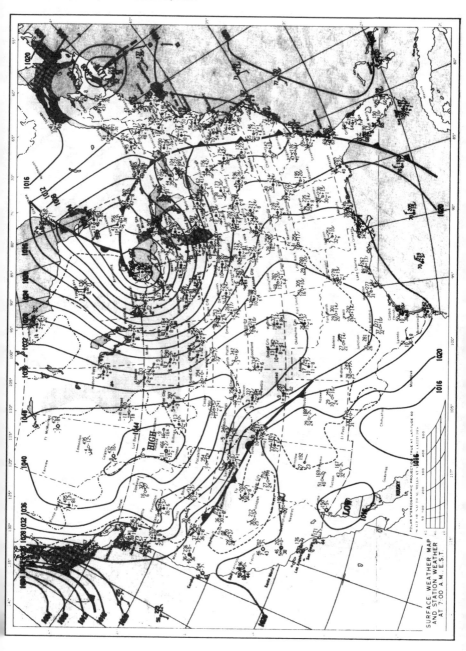

SURFACE WEATHER MAP
AND STATION WEATHER
AT 7:00 A.M. EST

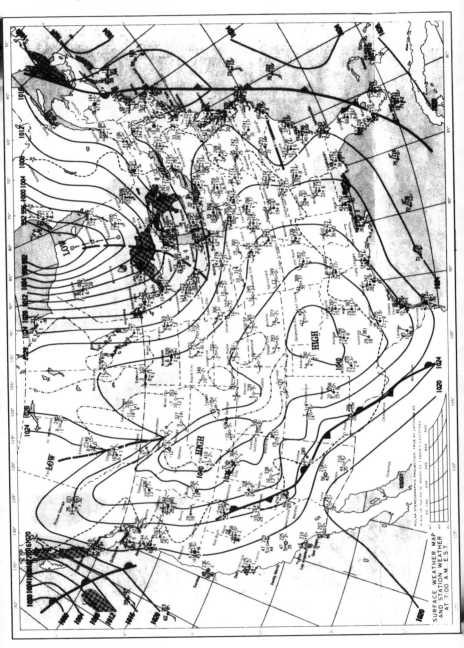

SURFACE WEATHER MAP
AND STATION WEATHER
AT 7:00 A.M. E.S.T.

Visit a Weather Office

The National Weather Service has more than 250 offices in the United States. You should be able to arrange a visit to one while you are working on your Weather merit badge requirements. Many television stations have weather broadcasters who might be willing to help. A nearby university or college with a meteorology or atmospheric science department might help you, as well. There also are many amateur weather observers who can show you the basic measurements, instruments, and weather charts.

The most obvious way to study the weather is to observe actual events and keep a record of what you see. Daily observations of temperature, wind, pressure, clouds, and rainfall can help you understand how the atmosphere behaves. Keep a daily weather log, similar to the one shown, for at least a week and preferably for a month or more. Make entries at the same time each day. You can obtain readings from your own instruments, from local television or radio, or from tuning to the NOAA Weather Radio broadcast in your area. By comparing readings from day to day, you can see how the various weather elements change at your location in response to passing weather systems.

DAILY WEATHER LOG
Observation time: _____

Date	Observed Weather	Temp.	Relative Humidity	Wind (Dir./speed)	Pressure	24-hr. Rainfall	Forecast for Tomorrow
1							
2							
3							
4							
5							
6							
7							
8							
9							

Make your own weather chart, using this form as a guide, for requirement 8a. Keep a 30-day record based on local weather forecasts and your own observations. Make and record observations at the same time each day.

Predicting the Weather

The whole of the atmosphere is involved in weather changes. To forecast the weather, a meteorologist must know conditions of temperature, pressure, humidity, and wind throughout the ocean of air, top to bottom and all over the planet. The meteorologist must know about the earth's water oceans as well as its ocean of air. Because it is hard to obtain information where no people live, such as over the oceans, there are many gaps in the knowledge used in weather forecasting.

The situation is better now than in the past. Early attempts to obtain weather data aloft were made using kites that carried recording instruments called *meteorographs*. Airplanes also were used to carry meteorographs. But in neither case could they be carried as high as the top of the troposphere. The information recorded on a meteorograph could not be used until the instrument was returned to a weather office.

The balloon-borne radiosonde changed all that. It was responsible for a revolution in understanding the atmosphere. By tracking the balloons, it became possible to measure wind speed and direction aloft, even where no clouds were present. The practical use of this ability did not become widespread until the development of radio direction-finding devices called *radiotheodolites*. A radiosonde with wind-measurement capability is known as a *rawinsonde*. Rawinsondes typically rise to well above the tropopause, so today it is common to have measurements of all the needed weather variables to heights up to about 100,000 feet.

Storm Detection and Tracking

The first weather satellite, known as TIROS-1, was launched in the spring of 1960. It was highly successful at giving meteorologists their first overall view of entire storm systems. TIROS satellites were polar orbiters, which means they passed overhead any one spot on the earth only twice a day. To get a broad view of the whole planet, several pictures had to be pieced together into a composite photograph. A major benefit from such satellites was that tropical cyclones at sea could be spotted and tracked long before they made dangerous landfalls. Before the age of satellites, meteorologists had to rely on reports from ships at sea that blundered into cyclones. Since 1960, no major tropical cyclone has struck without any warning.

When a satellite is launched into an orbit at the right height (about 22,000 miles) over the earth's equator, it orbits at exactly the same rate at which the earth rotates and thus remains fixed over the same spot. Such an orbit is called a *geosynchronous* orbit. From this lofty height, a satellite surveys a large region. The pictures taken over a period of time from such a satellite can be displayed in sequence to show the cloud motions. Satellite observations are especially important in areas where little or no other information is available, such as over the oceans.

Besides simply taking pictures, the newest geosynchronous satellites (called GOES—Geostationary Operational Environmental Satellite) can make sophisticated atmospheric measurements. These measurements allow meteorologists to estimate atmospheric temperature and water vapor content. It is expected that these measurements will become even more sophisticated in the future.

After World War II, observers noticed that weather seemed to affect radarscopes used for tracking airplanes. They decided that radar might be a good way to detect and track weather targets. The earliest weather radars were converted from military radars in the late 1940s. By 1960, weather radars were in widespread use for tracking precipitation. Basically, the radar beam is sent out from an antenna and is bounced back off of objects that the beam strikes. The reflected signal is amplified electronically and displayed in various ways. Radar signals are called "echoes" because of their similarity to an ordinary sound echo.

Recently, weather radars have begun to include *Doppler* equipment (named for the physicist Christian Doppler, who discovered the so-called *Doppler effect*). Doppler radars work like police radars to measure the speed of a target. They provide information about the speed of precipitation echoes along a radar beam. It helps meteorologists to have such information about motions within storms, especially severe thunderstorms that might contain tornadoes.

Doppler radar is a much-improved tool for detecting and recognizing dangerous weather.

Weather radar antenna, with a man standing next to it for scale. This example is a Doppler radar used for weather research.

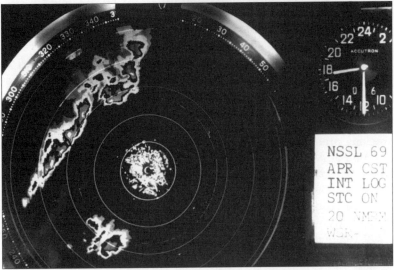

Example of a radar display, showing a line of thunderstorms northwest of the radar site (at the center) and an isolated thunderstorm ahead of the line, to the southwest of the radar. The storms occurred on April 6, 1969. The radar is located at the National Severe Storms Laboratory in Norman, Oklahoma.

Forecasting—Past and Present

Americans in earlier times didn't have much help from weather forecasters until the United States Weather Bureau (the predecessor to today's National Weather Service) became well established in the late 1800s. As often as not, farmers and sailors had to be their own forecasters. They used all kinds of natural signs as indicators. These included such short-term events as cloud patterns, dew on the grass, winds, and waves. For long-term indications, they studied the hair on caterpillars, the migration patterns of birds, or the hibernation of animals. Using such methods as these, forecasters could blame no one but themselves if something went wrong with their predictions.

In addition to the natural indicators, there were the almanacs. Predictions published in these books are very general and are based mostly on past weather history. Though their true value is controversial, almanacs have served as the only forecast source for many people through the ages and are still around today.

In recent years, there has been much improvement in science-based weather forecasting, both short-term and long-term. Much of this progress began with World War II. The vast wartime movements

A meteorologist with the National Weather Service uses a weather map from a numerical weather prediction model to help him prepare a forecast.

of ships, planes, and troops made it necessary for the armed services to have forecasts as accurate as possible far in advance. They set up their own meteorological groups and worked with the U.S. Weather Bureau and American universities to develop new techniques. Thousands of men and women received weather training. Many stayed in meteorology after the war and helped pioneer the peacetime application of new ideas.

The current explosion in electronics technology has made high-speed computers an everyday working tool in many areas, including weather forecasting. The computer made it possible to solve mathematical formulas and equations of meteorology that had been unsolvable before. A completely scientific means for weather forecasting became possible in the 1950s: the NWP models already mentioned. These models are being improved continually.

Climate

Weather is the condition of the atmosphere for a short time. *Climate* is the average of the weather over a longer time.

The word climate comes from the Greek word "klima," meaning angle. This name was used because the angle at which the sun strikes the earth largely determines the climate. At the equator, the sun is nearly straight overhead most of the year, so most of the equatorial region is hot. In the polar regions, the opposite is true. Poleward from the equator, the climate gradually shifts from hot to cold. In between are what we call the *temperate zones,* which include the United States.

Many other factors influence climate, of course. No definite rule can be made for a part of the world simply because it is a certain distance from the equator. Altitude affects climate, for example. In Peru at 10,000 to 15,000 feet above sea level, the sun can make it quite warm during the day but at night it gets cold. Many high peaks are snow-covered all year, despite their location close to the equator.

Ocean currents can make a major difference, as well. England is as far north as parts of Labrador and Newfoundland, but the warm waters of the Gulf Stream moderate the winters in England so that they are warmer on the average than those in New York City.

The Local Climate

Climate can have a large effect on agriculture and industry. It makes possible a great variety of foods and textiles. Wouldn't it be tiresome if the climate were the same the world over? Imagine having to eat coconuts and pineapple three times a day, or bean soup indefinitely! World trade would be of little use if all countries raised the same agricultural products. Vacation plans wouldn't be of much interest if people in hot countries could only travel to other hot countries.

Climatic differences make this an interesting and productive world. Study your own community. It probably owes much of its unique character to climate. If its chief products are agricultural,

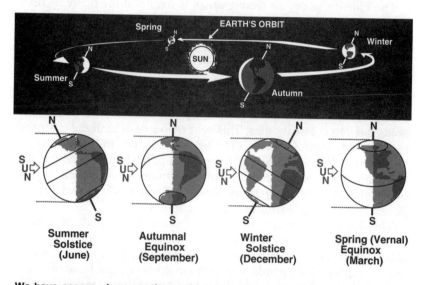

Summer Solstice (June)

Autumnal Equinox (September)

Winter Solstice (December)

Spring (Vernal) Equinox (March)

We have seasons because the earth's axis is tilted relative to the plane of its orbit around the sun. This tilt (about 23.5 degrees from the perpendicular) remains the same all year as seen from deep space (top), but changes relative to the sun (bottom). At the summer solstice (first day of summer, bottom left), the north pole tilts toward the sun, and the sun reaches its northernmost point in the sky. This is the longest day of the year in the northern hemisphere. The north pole is in constant daylight, while the south pole is in constant darkness. Everything is reversed at the winter solstice (first day of winter, bottom, second from right). The south pole tilts toward the sun, and the southern hemisphere has long days and warm weather as the sun appears at its southernmost point in the sky. In between, during the autumnal equinox and spring equinox, sunshine is evenly distributed across both hemispheres.

you can be sure it does. If they are industrial, where does the power come from? Where do the raw materials come from? If water transportation is important to the local economy, that requires plenty of rainfall or an ice-free port in winter.

Do you live in a resort or vacation area? Then your community depends heavily on climate. People probably wouldn't vacation in the far north without the many lakes and forests made possible by lots of rain and snow, or the chance for winter sports like skiing.

Climate affects everyday living conditions. Study your house. It's usual for a home in the north to have a furnace, storm windows, and a peaked roof to shed snow. A southern home might not need a furnace, but it might have an air conditioner. It might have a flat or low roof and specially treated wood to resist moisture or insects.

The climate in dry or desert areas is healthful for many. People are attracted there as tourists or retirees. Others go in search of mineral wealth. Minerals are washed down into some dry areas by flash floods from the mountains and deposited where they are fairly easy to recover.

Studying the climate is vital in locating industries and other commercial or agricultural enterprises. It is possible to get records from the National Climatic Data Center on average weather conditions going back to colonial times. This vast resource of material is stored in Asheville, North Carolina. (The address is given in the Resources section that follows.) Much of it has been published on a city, state, national, and worldwide basis covering many years. Much of this material is available at National Weather Service offices and at public and university libraries across the country.

This long-term climatic information shows the climate of a location or region and helps agricultural, commercial, industrial, and other interests in planning. If a city's records, for instance, show mostly calm or light winds, the area would be a poor location for a factory that produces air pollutants. Climatic summaries help in planning the location of resort hotels and business ventures. They help in deciding when and where to go on vacation or to retire. They tell the most likely time of favorable weather in planning an outdoor event.

They help farmers know the best time to plant and harvest crops, dry hay or raisins, or cure tobacco. They suggest the chances for hail, droughts, and freezes at any location. They're also useful in laying out airport runways and in determining the amount of heat or refrigeration needed for a house or factory or for the shipment of perishable foods.

Masters of ships at sea consult climatic charts to learn of the wind, ocean currents, and storm tracks. Climatic records may be introduced as evidence in court to clarify the causes of accidents on highways, in the air, and at sea. Climate affects people's moods, health, and social behavior and agricultural, commercial, and industrial pursuits the world over.

Future Climate and You

An important thing to think about is the effect present human activities can have on future climatic conditions. In some areas of the world, wasteful and thoughtless human actions have had a clearly negative impact on the local climate. For example, the work of archaeologists has shown that many areas that now are deserts once were fertile and productive. This is true of many countries around the Mediterranean Sea and the Arabian Desert.

The biblical "land of milk and honey" north of Egypt and Egypt itself once had lush fields, orchards, and gardens. Careless agricultural methods allowed the topsoil to be washed away. Loss of green plants cut down on evaporation or transpiration. A cycle began that produced parched soil, sand dunes, and scant rainfall. Similar things have happened in the United States, such as during the "Dust Bowl" era of the 1930s, but changes in agricultural methods might have kept the effects from becoming permanent.

Industrial pollutants and automobile exhaust have contributed to the growing problem of *acid rain.* This is rain that has become acidic from absorbing certain types of pollutants. Acid rain can destroy life in lakes and rivers, which can have a damaging effect on the hydrologic cycle.

Recently, the world has become aware of the threat of so-called *greenhouse gases* given off by human activities. The most notable is the carbon dioxide given off when burning fossil fuels like coal and oil. Another source of carbon dioxide is burning trees in the rain forests of the world as large areas are cleared to make room for agriculture.

Although meteorologists and climatologists do not know exactly what effect the greenhouse gases will have, it appears that excess carbon dioxide and other gases might trap the earth's heat and cause the climate all over the globe to warm up. Global warming could have disastrous effects on agriculture. Areas of productive farmland could become desert.

The atmosphere and the oceans together are a highly complex system. They are not yet so well understood that we can predict the effects, but there is clear agreement that atmospheric carbon dioxide is increasing rapidly.

Another concern is the loss of ozone in the stratosphere. Damage to the ozone appears to be the result of chemicals called *chlorofluorocarbons* (or CFCs) that have been used as propellant in aerosol cans, as refrigerants in air conditioners, and as solvents in certain industrial processes. As you have seen, ozone in the stratosphere acts to screen people (and all other forms of life on earth) from the sun's harmful ultraviolet radiation. The ultimate effect of the loss of ozone on the climate and living things is unknown.

In general, conservation of resources can be of long-term benefit by lessening the effects of human activities on the global climate. Recycling and not wasting energy can reduce the rate of loss of the world's resources and cut pollution due to manufacturing. Water conservation and careful agricultural and mining practices can preserve the natural balance of things.

Continued exploitation and waste can cost much more in the long run than developing conservation practices today. It is up to you to continue improving upon conservation methods that will protect the earth's temperate and beneficial climate.

Weather Resources

Scouting Literature

Agribusiness, Aviation, Chemistry, Electricity, Emergency Preparedness, Environmental Science, Geology, Oceanography, and *Soil and Water Conservation* merit badge pamphlets

Books

Anderson, Bette R. *Weather in the West.* American West Publishing, 1975. A description of weather events common to the western United States, with many photographs, including color.

Anthes, Richard A., Hans A. Panofsky, John J. Cahir, and Albert Rango. *The Atmosphere.* Merrill, 1975. An introductory textbook with many illustrations and photographs.

Battan, Louis J. *Fundamentals of Meteorology.* Prentice-Hall, 1979. An introductory textbook with many illustrations and photographs.

Cotton, William R. *Storms.* Aster Press, 1990. A detailed, nontechnical look at many different kinds of storms, including who studies them and how they are investigated scientifically.

Keen, Richard A. *Skywatch: The Western Weather Guide.* Fulcrum, 1987. Descriptions and explanations of weather in the western United States, using photographs, diagrams, and satellite images.

Kocin, Paul J., and Louis W. Uccellini. *Snowstorms Along the Northeastern Coast of the United States: 1955 to 1985.* American Meteorological Society, 1990. Detailed, somewhat technical documentation of twenty major snowfall events, with weather charts, diagrams, photographs, and satellite pictures.

Neiburger, Morris, James G. Edinger, and William D. Bonner. *Understanding Our Atmospheric Environment.* W.H. Freeman, 1982. An introductory textbook for college freshmen; also accessible to the high school student.

Schaefer, Vincent J. *A Field Guide to the Atmosphere.* American Meteorological Society, 1981. Practical material for anyone interested in the weather.

Scorer, Richard, and Arjen Verkaik. *Spacious Skies.* American Meteorological Society, 1989. Loaded with photographs, many in color, and descriptive text.

Uman, Martin A. *Understanding Lightning.* Bek Technical Publications, 1971. Facts about lightning, including a discussion of lightning myths and misunderstandings; many photographs.

National Weather Service Publications

The following are prepared by the National Weather Service. Many have been prepared jointly with the Federal Emergency Management Agency (FEMA) and the American Red Cross. Most of these documents can be obtained from your local National Weather Service office at little or no charge, or by writing to the Superintendent of Documents, U.S. Government Printing Office, Washington, D.C. 20402.

Floods, Flash Floods, and Warnings. Includes descriptions of floods and flash floods, their associated dangers, and flood safety rules.

Spotters' Guide for Identifying and Reporting Severe Local Storms. Descriptions of cloud formations associated with severe local storms, designed to accompany training programs for severe storm spotters.

Storm Surge and Hurricane Safety. Definitions and descriptions of weather hazards related to tropical cyclones, and safety rules.

Includes a tracking chart for North Atlantic hurricanes and tropical storms.

Thunderstorms and Lightning. Descriptions of thunderstorms, their attendant weather hazards, and safety rules.

Tornado Safety—Surviving Nature's Most Violent Storm. Tornado facts, statistics, and safety rules.

Winter Storms: A Guide for Survival. Summary of winter weather hazards, including definitions, safety rules, and other information.

Other Publications and Periodicals

"Clouds: A Guide to the Sky." Cloud chart showing photographic examples of the primary cloud types. Available from Sky Guide, P.O. Box 30027, Greenwood Station, Seattle, WA 98103-0027.

Daily Weather Maps. Published weekly by the Climate Analysis Center, World Weather Building, Washington DC 20233.

Local Climatological Data. Monthly summaries of weather data from states and local areas. Check with your local National Weather Service office for availability or contact the National Climatic Data Center, Federal Building, Asheville, NC 28801-2696.

Storm Data. A monthly record of significant and unusual weather events. Includes photographs and charts related to major storm events, with descriptions and detailed information about damage and casualties from each state. Available from the National Climatic Data Center (see above).

Weatherwise. A bimonthly magazine about weather for all levels of interest. Published by Heldref Publications in association with the American Meteorological Society.

Acknowledgments

The Boy Scouts of America is grateful to Dr. Charles A. Doswell III, National Severe Storms Laboratory, Norman, Oklahoma, and Michael L. Branick, National Weather Service, Experimental Forecast Facility, Norman, Oklahoma, for their assistance in the preparation of this new edition of the *Weather* merit badge pamphlet.

Photo Credits

Cover and pages 52, 66, and 67, C. Doswell
   [balloon, radar, and man at computer]
Page 24, C. Knight, National Center for Atmospheric Research
   [hailstone cross section]
Pages 32 and 66, National Severe Storms Laboratory
   [tornado and radar display]

NOTES

NOTES

NOTES

NOTES